10
c

50¢
14x

Wings

Also by Arthur Kopit

Oh Dad, Poor Dad, Mamma's Hung You in the Closet
and I'm Feelin' So Sad

The Day the Whores Came Out to Play Tennis
and Other Plays

Indians

Wings

A play by Arthur Kopit

A Mermaid Dramabook

Hill and Wang   New York

A division of Farrar, Straus and Giroux

Library of Congress Cataloging in Publication Data

Kopit, Arthur L.   Wings: a play.
(A Mermaid dramabook)
1. Stroke patients—Rehabilitation—Drama. I. Title.
PS3521.0573W5 1978   812'.5'4   78-10428
ISBN 0-8090-9756-1
ISBN 0-8090-1239-1 pbk.

Wings was originally commissioned by Earplay,
the drama project of National Public Radio.

Preface

In the fall of 1976, I was commissioned to write an original radio play for Earplay, the drama project of National Public Radio. They did not stipulate what the play should be about, only that it should not last longer than an hour. *Wings* was the result. It has since, of course, been altered and expanded, mainly to accommodate the visual components of my central character's condition. But the play was, and still remains, essentially about language disorder and its implications. For that reason, radio was the perfect initial medium; it did not permit me to get lost in the myriad and always fascinating perceptual aberrations that can accompany any severe damage to the brain. I now believe that if I had conceived *Wings* directly for the stage instead, I would have inevitably found myself seduced by the stage's greater freedom into investigating at length these astonishing but ultimately peripheral aspects of aphasia. Most likely, more characters would have been introduced, a welter of extraordinary syndromes revealed and examined. If brain damage is terrifying to behold, it is also alluring. One feels the need to avert one's eyes and hide, and the equal if not greater need to keep looking. It is a very scary business, this job of exploring who we are. Very quickly, I suspect, my focus would have vanished. All of which is to say that if *Wings* exhibits in its present form any excellence of vision and craft, that excellence is without question a direct function of the rigor imposed on it by its initial incarnation. For that reason, I must express a deep debt of gratitude to Earplay for having commissioned this play, and particularly to the man who directed both its initial version and its first production on the stage at Yale, John Madden.

There is a question which I suspect must arise inevitably in the mind of anyone who reads or sees this play: to what degree is *Wings* faithful to fact, to what degree sheer speculation.

In the spring of 1976, seven months before Earplay was to commission me to write on a subject of my choosing, my father suffered a major stroke which rendered him incapable of speech. Furthermore, because of certain other

complications, all related to his aphasia, and all typical of
stroke, it was impossible to know how much he
comprehended. Certainly there was no doubt that his
capacity to comprehend had been drastically impaired and
reduced. As best I could, I tried to understand what he was
going through. It seemed to me that, regardless of how
reduced his senses were, the isolation he was being forced
to endure had to verge on the intolerable; clearly, he had not
lost all comprehension—the look of terror in his eyes was
unmistakable. Yet, not only did he tolerate this state; every
now and then, if one watched carefully enough, something
escaped from this shell that was his body and his prison,
something almost but not quite palpable, something not
readily brought to the attention of a nurse (I tried it once but
she saw nothing), something which I felt possessed a kind of
glow or flicker, rather like a lamp way off in the dark,
something only barely perceptible. I took these faint flashes
to be him signaling. And although I allowed for the possibility
that what I was perceiving was nothing but mirage, or the
mirrored reflections of my own hopeful and constant
signalings to him, nonetheless, it seemed to me (indeed,
seemed irrefutable) that in some ineffably essential way,
reduced as he was, he was still the same person he had
been. This thought was both heartening and frightful. To
what extent was he still intact? To what extent was he aware
of what had befallen him? *What was it like inside?*

And then Earplay came along. By its very nature, radio
seemed to offer an especially appropriate means of exploring
these particular questions.

I recognized at once that I could not deal directly with my
father. For one thing, I was too close to him to hold any
hope of objectivity. For another, his case was too severe, too
grim, my audience would turn away. So I looked elsewhere
for a model. The questions would remain the same, of
course, and just as valid; my understanding of my father's
world would have to come—if indeed it could at all—through
analogy. I decided to focus on two patients I had met at the
Burke Rehabilitation Center in White Plains, New York, where

my father had been transferred after his stay in the hospital. Both were women: one was old, in her late seventies, perhaps older; the other, not quite thirty. Like my father, both had suffered major strokes, though neither was as incapacitated as he; both at least could talk. Certainly they could not talk well.

The speech of the younger woman was fluent and possessed normal intonations, cadence, and syntactical structure—in fact, to such an extent that anyone who did not understand English would have sworn she was making sense. Nonetheless, her sentences were laced with a kind of babbled jargon so that, by and large, she made no sense at all. In her early stages, she seemed unaware of this appalling deficit.* In contrast, the older woman's words had no fluency, no melodic inflection, no syntactical richness. Her words emerged with difficulty and sounded like something composed for a telegram. Modifiers and conjunctions for the most part were absent. But at least her words made sense. The problem was, as often as not, the sense they conveyed was not the sense she intended. Though she usually was aware of these "mistakes," or at least could be made aware of them, she could not prevent them from occurring. Neither could she readily correct them. Aside from her aphasia, each woman was relatively free of other symptoms.

I had met the older woman while accompanying my father one afternoon on his rounds. When he went down for speech therapy, she was one of the three other patients in the room. I had never observed a speech therapy session before and was nervous. The day, I recall vividly, was warm, humid. The windows of the room were open. A scent of flowers suffused the air. To get the session started, the therapist asked the older woman if she could name the seasons of the year. With much effort, she did, though not in

*This particular kind of speech, typical of a certain form of aphasia, is characterized by neologisms, and sounds very much like double talk or gibberish. The word *gibberish,* however, suggests psychosis and dementia, and is therefore inappropriate for describing an effect of organic brain disease; the term *jargonaphasia* is used instead.

proper order. She seemed annoyed with herself for having any difficulty at all with such a task. The therapist then asked her which of these seasons corresponded to the present. The woman turned at once to the window. She could see the garden, the flowers. Her eyes were clear, alert; there was no question but that she understood what was wanted. I cannot remember having ever witnessed such an intense struggle. At first, she did nothing but sit calmly and wait for the word to arrive on its own. When it didn't, she tried to force the word out by herself, through thinking; as if to assist what clearly was a process of expulsion, she scrunched her face up, squeezed her eyelids shut. But no word emerged. Physically drained, her face drenched with sweat, she tried another trick: she cocked her head and listened to the birds, whose sound was incessant. When this too led to nothing, she sniffed the air. When nothing came of this strategy either, she turned her attention to what she was wearing, a light cotton dress; she even touched the fabric. Finally, something connected. Her lips began to form a word. She shut her eyes. Waited. The word emerged. *Winter.*

When informed that it was summer she seemed astonished, how was it possible? . . . a mistake like that . . . obviously she knew what season it was, anyone with eyes could tell at once what season it was! . . . and yet . . . She looked over at where I sat and shook her head in dismay, then laughed and said, "This is really nuts, isn't it!"

I sat there, stunned. I could not believe that anyone making a mistake of such gross proportions and with such catastrophic implications could laugh at it.

So there would be no misunderstanding, the therapist quickly pointed out that this mistake stemmed completely from her stroke; in no way was she demented. The woman smiled (she knew all that) and turned away, stared back out the window at the garden. *This is really nuts, isn't it!*—I could not get her phrase from my mind. In its intonation, it had conveyed no feeling of anger, resignation, or despair. Rather, it had conveyed amazement, and in that amazement, a trace

(incredible as it seemed) of delight. This is not to suggest
that anyone witnessing this incident could, even for an
instant, have imagined that she was in any sense pleased
with her condition. The amazement, and its concomitant
delight, seemed to me to reflect only an acknowledgment
that her condition was extraordinary, and in no way denied or
obviated the terror or the horror that were at its core. By
some (I supposed) nourishing spring of inner strength and
light, of whose source I had no idea, she had come to a
station in her life from which she could perceive in what was
happening something that bore the aspect of adventure, and
it was through this perhaps innate capacity to perceive and
appreciate adventure, and perhaps in this sense only, that
she found some remaining modicum of delight, which I
suspect kept her going. Of course, all this was speculation.
As I said, I was stunned. The therapist asked her to try again
and she did. And she got it—summer! With great excitement,
she tried once again. Same result. She had it! Summer! She
tried again. *Winter.* It was lost. She heard but could do
nothing. She shook her head in consternation. Smiled in
wonderment. In the course of the session, I discovered we
shared the same birthday.

Later that afternoon, I inquired as to who she was, and was
told she was a former aviatrix and wing-walker. I believe my
response to this news was *"What?"*—although I think I may
have said, *"Wing-walker?"* Either way, my composure was
slipping. I felt decidedly inadequate.

A nurse brought me to her room (she was out, gone down to
dinner) and showed me a photograph pinned up on her wall;
it had been taken when she was in her twenties. In the
photograph, a biplane sits on a large grassy field, a crowded
grandstand in the distance, its front railing draped with flags.
The plane is a Curtiss Jenny. A pilot sits in the rearmost of
its two open cockpits; she is standing out on its lower wing,
white silk scarf around her neck, goggles set back on top of
her leather helmet. She wears jodhpurs, boots, a leather
jacket. Her face is lean and handsome and imperious. The
same noble and slightly quizzical smile I'd seen that

afternoon is there. Her right hand is holding on to the wire stays behind her. The propeller is spinning; apparently, her plane is about to take off. Several nurses come in and join us in staring at the photograph. Her eyes seem on fire; they are filled with an unquenchable eager passion. Her left hand is waving toward the camera and the unseen throng.

Needless to say, had I invented her, the invention would have been excessive, would have strained credulity—only in dreams and fiction did one meet persons such as this. Yet, here she was, she existed. Everyone at Burke who knew her agreed that the fortitude and *esprit* I'd seen that afternoon in the therapy session were no aberration. By nature she was one of the bravest, most extraordinary persons they had ever met. There was no other choice: she was my model.

With that decision, a task that might otherwise have been little more than grim took on the aspects of an adventure. As scrupulously as possible, I would try to explore, through her mind, this terrible and awesome realm of being. Surely, that realm bore resemblance to my father's. Courage was not her quality alone.

The title came at once. Also, with it, two recognitions: if *Wings* was to be effective, it would have to deal specifically with its central character and not with some general condition called stroke; at the same time, to be effective, it would have to possess an absolutely solid clinical accuracy.

To these ends, I began an exhaustive study of airplanes and brain damage—unquestionably a weird conjunction of subjects. The study of airplanes was simple. Libraries provided everything I had to know about early aviation—how the old biplanes were flown, who flew them, what their cockpits looked like, felt like; and especially about that remarkable post-World War I phenomenon known as barnstorming, when pilots (many of them women) toured the country, thrilling crowds with exhibitions of their marvelous, death-defying daring and skill. Burke was where I went to study brain damage and rehabilitation.

It quickly became clear that, for my purposes at least, the speech patterns of this older woman (due to the nature of her stroke) were not as varied and therefore not as interesting as the speech patterns of many other patients.

For greater linguistic richness, I turned to the patient in her late twenties as the principal model for my central character's speech. In her own right, this young woman was as exceptional as the older. Certainly she was no less brave. When I met her, she was able to acknowledge the gravity of her condition, and fought all tendencies to self-pity and despair. With as much cheerfulness as she could muster (her capacity for hope seemed limitless), she worked every moment that she could at the one task in her life that mattered: the reassembling of her shattered world. But there was yet another exceptional aspect to this young woman, and in truth it was this that made me turn to her as the model not only for my central character's patterns of speech but, in fact, ultimately, her very processes of thought: *she was left-handed*. From this one seemingly insignificant trait, many remarkable abilities derived.

In a right-handed person, the left hemisphere of the cerebral cortex is dominant and controls all activities connected with speech and analytic consciousness. However, for persons who are by nature left-handed, some of the left hemisphere's usual functions are taken over by the normally nonverbal and intuitive right. Should such a person suffer a stroke or injury to the left cerebral hemisphere, he stands a good chance of retaining a degree of verbal lucidity and insight inaccessible to those whose left hemisphere maintains sole dominance. This was the case with the young woman I met at Burke. Because of her left-handedness, she possessed the rare ability to recognize and articulate, to a slight but still significant extent, her own patterns of thought. Repeatedly, she would describe a certain dividedness within her head, as if she literally sensed the separate hemispheres at work, usually in contradiction to each other. In such instances, she would actually refer to her mind's "two sides," and frequently accompany this description with a slicing gesture of her hand, clearly suggestive of a vertically symmetrical division of her entire body. Once, she described coming to a large puddle. With great amusement she recounted how one side of her head told her to go left, while the other side told her to go right; to end the controversy and resolve the debate, she walked through the middle.

At Burke I studied her attempts at keeping a journal, listened to hours of taped interviews between her and her speech therapist, and of course, as often as possible, talked directly to her myself. She seemed to understand something of my project and its purposes, and seemed pleased that somehow she could be of help. Gradually, an image of a remarkable and quite vivid interior landscape began to form in my mind, frightening and awesome in its details, its blatant gaps, its implications.

But there was still another person crucial to my research: her therapist, Jacqueline Doolittle. Her knowledge of aphasia was my touchstone. At all hours of the day and sometimes night, I would call Mrs. Doolittle with some generally naïve question about the brain, and she, with limitless good humor, would set me straight. It is both astonishing and humbling the number of assumptions one can make in this field which are absolutely wrong. Nonetheless, I kept phoning and, if not phoning, stopping by her office, usually unannounced. To her credit, and perhaps to mine, she never threw me out. Gradually, things became clearer. I should point out, Mrs. Doolittle's understanding of aphasia went far beyond the clinical: Jacqueline Doolittle had herself been aphasic once.

Her aphasia had resulted from a head injury sustained in an auto accident. Eventually she recovered, and her recollections of this period are like visions of a sojourn in another realm: vivid and detailed. Without a doubt, it was this experience that lay at the root of her exceptional empathic abilities as a therapist.

What she described was a world of fragments, a world without dimension, a world where time meant nothing constant, and from which there seemed no method of escape. She thought she had either gone mad or been captured by an unknown enemy for purposes she could not fathom, and in fact took the hospital she was in to be a farmhouse in disguise, controlled by her captors. For a long time, she was unable to distinguish that the words she spoke were jargon, and wondered why everyone she saw spoke to her in a foreign tongue. Her state was one of utter isolation, confusion, terror, and disarray. She wondered if perhaps she was dreaming. Sometimes the thought occurred to her that she was dead. Then, very gradually, the swelling in her head subsided, and little by little the cells in her left cerebral hemisphere began to make their proper neural connections. She began to understand what people said. When she spoke, the right words, as if by magic, started flowing. She returned to the world she knew. *Wings* owes much of its structure and detail to these recollections.

How much of this play, then, is speculation?

Wings is a play about a woman whom I have called Emily Stilson. Though she suffers a stroke, in no way is it a case study, and in its execution I have assiduously avoided any kind of clinical or documentary approach. Indeed, it has been so conceived and constructed that its audience can, for the most part, observe this realm that she is in only through her own consciousness. In short, *Wings* is a work of speculation informed by fact.

But any attempt to render a person's consciousness through words, even autobiography, must be speculative. Where thoughts are concerned, there are no infallible reporters. What we remember of our pasts is filtered by our sensibilities and predilections, and can as easily be imaginary as real. To what extent did Jacqui Doolittle remember only what she wanted to? To what extent did her mind, in its damaged state, withhold from her consciousness something essential to her experience? Given that she was suffering a severe language deficit, how much can we trust her verbal recollections? In this arena, hard facts do not exist. Yet, if we cannot hope for what is provable, we at least can strive for what is plausible. By any criteria, Jacqui Doolittle's account has emotional validity. The same holds true for the young left-handed woman's. It was this emotional truth, informed by fact, that I was after. So far as I was able, I have avoided in this play any colorations of my own and, as far as I know, have attributed to Emily Stilson no symptoms that are unlikely or impossible. Though Emily Stilson is a composite of many persons, and derives finally from my imagination, I have worked as if in fact she existed, and in this light, and within the limitations of this form, have felt myself obliged to render her condition as it was, not as I might have preferred it.

There are two books whose influence on me I would like to acknowledge, and which I strongly recommend to anyone interested in further explorations of this subject: Howard Gardner's *The Shattered Mind,* and A. R. Luria's *The Man with a Shattered World.*

I would also like to acknowledge the crucial role of Robert Brustein, as Dean of the Yale School of Drama, in the evolution of this play. Mr. Brustein had heard the radio play performed, and had expressed his admiration of the work. In November of 1977, he called me to say that he had been thinking about the play, and had come to believe it could be even more effective on the stage. A slot had opened in the Yale Rep's spring schedule. Was I interested?

Not only was I interested, I was flabbergasted. Since summer, when I had first heard *Wings* performed, I had been trying to figure out if it was possible to adapt it to the stage. The problems, it turned out, were considerable, both structurally and thematically. That afternoon, indeed less than an hour before the call came in, I had suddenly realized how to do it.

For those who may have missed the issue, *Forbes Magazine* ranks playwrighting extremely low on the list of Easy Ways to

Earn One's Fortune. In fact, it is no simple matter to earn one's living at its practice. I would therefore like to express both my family's and my deep gratitude to the Rockefeller Foundation for a generous and timely grant, which alone enabled me to devote, with ease of mind, the enormous time and energy that I soon found the work demanded, both in the writing and in the research.

For their extensive and always generous assistance in that research, I am profoundly indebted and grateful to the Burke Rehabilitation Center; and especially to Jacqueline Doolittle.

A.L.K.

Wings was given its first stage performance at the Yale Repertory Theatre in New Haven, Connecticut, on March 3, 1978, with the following cast:

EMILY STILSON	Constance Cummings
AMY	Marianne Owen
DOCTORS	Geoffrey Pierson
	Roy Steinberg
NURSES	Caris Corfman
	Carol Ostrow
BILLY	Richard Grusin
MR. BROWNSTEIN	Ira Bernstein
MRS. TIMMINS	Betty Pelzer
Directed by	John Madden
Designed by	Andrew Jackness
Costumes by	Jeanne Button
Lighting by	Tom Schraeder
Sound by	Tom Voegeli
Music by	Herb Pilhofer

I weave in and out of the strange clouds, hidden in my tiny cockpit, submerged, alone, on the magnitude of this weird, unhuman space, venturing where man has never been, perhaps never meant to go. Am I myself a living, breathing, earth-bound body, or is this a dream of death I'm passing through? Am I alive, or am I really dead, a spirit in a spirit world. Am I actually in a plane, or have I crashed on some worldly mountain, and is this the afterlife?

Charles Lindbergh, *The Spirit of St. Louis.*

Wings

Characters

Emily Stilson
Amy, a therapist
Doctors
Nurses
Billy, a patient
Mr. Brownstein, a patient
Mrs. Timmins, a patient

The play takes place over a period of two years; it should be performed without intermission

Notes on the production of this play

The stage as a void.

System of black scrim panels that can move silently and easily, creating the impression of featureless, labyrinthine corridors.

Some panels mirrored so they can fracture light, create the impression of endlessness, even airiness, multiply and confuse images, confound one's sense of space.

Sound both live and pre-recorded, amplified; speakers all around the theater.

No attempt should be made to create a literal representation of Mrs. Stilson's world, especially since Mrs. Stilson's world is no longer in any way literal.

The scenes should blend. No clear boundaries or domains in time or space for Mrs. Stilson any more.

It is posited by this play that the woman we see in the center of the void is the intact inner self of Mrs. Stilson. This inner self does not need to move physically when her external body (which we cannot see) moves. Thus, we infer movement from the context; from whatever clues we can obtain. It is the same for her, of course. She learns as best she can.

And yet, sometimes, the conditions change; then the woman we observe is Mrs. Stilson as others see her. We thus infer who it is we are seeing from the context, too. Sometimes we see both the inner and outer self at once.

Nothing about her world is predictable or consistent. This fact is its essence.

The progression of the play is from fragmentation to integration. By the end, boundaries have become somewhat clearer. But she remains always in another realm from us.

Prelude

AS AUDIENCE ENTERS, A COZY ARMCHAIR VISIBLE
DOWNSTAGE IN A POOL OF LIGHT, DARKNESS
SURROUNDING IT.

A CLOCK HEARD TICKING IN THE DARK.

LIGHTS TO BLACK.

HOLD.

WHEN THE LIGHTS COME BACK, EMILY STILSON, A
WOMAN WELL INTO HER SEVENTIES, IS SITTING IN THE
ARMCHAIR READING A BOOK. SOME DISTANCE AWAY, A
FLOOR LAMP GLOWS DIMLY. ON THE OTHER SIDE OF
HER CHAIR, ALSO SOME DISTANCE AWAY, A SMALL
TABLE WITH A CLOCK. THE CHAIR, THE LAMP, AND THE
TABLE WITH THE CLOCK ALL SIT ISOLATED IN NARROW
POOLS OF LIGHT, DARKNESS BETWEEN AND AROUND
THEM.

THE CLOCK SEEMS TO BE TICKING A TRIFLE LOUDER
THAN NORMAL.

MRS. STILSON, ENJOYING HER BOOK AND THE
PLEASANT EVENING, READS ON SERENELY.

AND THEN SHE LOOKS UP.

THE LAMP DISAPPEARS INTO THE DARKNESS.

BUT SHE TURNS BACK TO HER BOOK AS IF NOTHING
ODD HAS HAPPENED; RESUMES READING.

AND THEN, A MOMENT LATER, SHE LOOKS UP AGAIN,
AN EXPRESSION OF SLIGHT PERPLEXITY ON HER FACE.
FOR NO DISCERNIBLE REASON, SHE TURNS TOWARD
THE CLOCK.

THE CLOCK AND THE TABLE IT IS SITTING ON
DISAPPEAR INTO THE DARKNESS.

SHE TURNS FRONT. STARES OUT INTO SPACE.

THEN SHE TURNS BACK TO HER BOOK. RESUMES
READING. BUT THE READING SEEMS AN EFFORT; HER
MIND IS ON OTHER THINGS.

THE CLOCK SKIPS A BEAT.

ONLY AFTER THE CLOCK HAS RESUMED ITS NORMAL
RHYTHM DOES SHE LOOK UP. IT IS AS IF THE SKIPPED
BEAT HAS ONLY JUST THEN REGISTERED. FOR THE
FIRST TIME, SHE DISPLAYS WHAT ONE MIGHT CALL
CONCERN.

AND THEN THE CLOCK STOPS AGAIN. THIS TIME THE
INTERVAL LASTS LONGER.

THE BOOK SLIPS OUT OF MRS. STILSON'S HANDS; SHE
STARES OUT IN TERROR.

BLACKOUT.

NOISE.

The moment of a stroke, even a relatively minor one, and its immediate aftermath, are an experience in chaos. Nothing at all makes sense. Nothing except perhaps this overwhelming disorientation will be remembered by the victim. The stroke usually happens suddenly. It is a catastrophe.

It is my intention that the audience recognize that some real event is occurring; that real information is being received by the victim, but that it is coming in too scrambled and too fast to be properly decoded. Systems overload.

And so this section must not seem like utter "noise," though certainly it must be more noisy than intelligible. I do not believe there is any way to be true to this material if it is not finally "composed" in rehearsal, on stage, by "feel." Theoretically, any sound or image herein described can occur anywhere in this section. The victim cannot process. Her familiar world has been rearranged. The puzzle is in pieces. All at once, and with no time to prepare, she has been picked up and dropped into another realm.

In order that this section may be put together in rehearsal (there being no one true "final order" to the images and sounds she perceives), I have divided this section into three discrete parts with the understanding that in performance these parts will blend together to form one cohesive whole.

The first group consists of the visual images Mrs. Stilson perceives.

The second group consists of those sounds emanating outside herself. Since these sounds are all filtered by her mind, and since her mind has been drastically altered, the question of whether we in the audience are hearing what is actually occurring or only hearing what she believes is occurring is unanswerable.

The third group contains Mrs. Stilson's words: the words she thinks and the words she speaks. Since we are perceiving the world through Mrs. Stilson's senses, there is no sure way for us to know whether she is actually saying any of these words aloud.

Since the experience we are exploring is not one of logic but its opposite, there is no logical reason for these groupings to occur in the order in which I have presented them. These are but components, building blocks, and can therefore be repeated, spliced, reversed, filtered, speeded up or slowed down. What should determine their final sequence and juxtaposition, tempi, intensity, is the "musical" sense of this section as a whole; it must pulse and build. An explosion quite literally is occurring in her brain, or rather, a series of explosions: the victim's mind, her sense of time and place, her sense of self, all are being shattered if not annihilated. Fortunately, finally, she will pass out. Were her head a pinball game it would register TILT—game over—stop. Silence. And resume again. Only now the victim is in yet another realm. The Catastrophe section is the journey or the fall into this strange and dreadful realm.

In the world into which Mrs. Stilson has been so violently and suddenly transposed, time and place are without definition. The distance from her old familiar world is immense. For all she knows, she could as well be on another planet.

In this new world, she moves from one space or thought or concept to another without willing or sometimes even knowing it. Indeed, when she moves in this maze-like place, it is as if the world around her and not she were doing all the moving. To her, there is nothing any more that is commonplace or predictable. Nothing is as it was. Everything comes as a surprise. Something has relieved her of command. Something beyond her comprehension has her in its grip.

In the staging of this play, the sense should therefore be conveyed of physical and emotional separation (by the use, for example, of the dark transparent screens through which her surrounding world can be only dimly and partly seen, or *by alteration of external sound) and of total immersion in strangeness.*

Because our focus is on Mrs. Stilson's inner self, it is important that she exhibit no particular overt physical disabilities. Furthermore, we should never see her in a wheelchair, even though, were we able to observe her through the doctors' eyes, a wheelchair is probably what she would, more often than not, be in.

One further note: because Mrs. Stilson now processes information at a different rate from us, there is no reason that what we see going on around her has to be the visual equivalent of what we hear.

Catastrophe

Images	Sounds outside herself
	(SOUNDS live or on tape, altered or unadorned)
	Of wind.
Mostly, it is whiteness. Dazzling, blinding.	Of someone breathing with effort, unevenly.
	Of something ripping, like a sheet.
Occasionally, there are brief rhombs of color, explosions of color, the color red being dominant.	Of something flapping, the sound suggestive of an old screen door perhaps, or a sheet or sail in the wind. It is a rapid fibrillation. And it is used mostly to mark transitions. It can seem ominous or not.
The mirrors, of course, reflect infinitely. Sense of endless space, endless corridors.	Of a woman's scream (though this sound should be altered by filters so it resembles other things, such as sirens).
	Of random noises recorded in a busy city hospital, then altered so as to be only minimally recognizable.
Nothing seen that is not a fragment. Every aspect of her world has been shattered.	Of a car's engine at full speed.
	Of a siren (altered to resemble a woman screaming).
Utter isolation.	Of an airplane coming closer, thundering overhead, then zooming off into silence.

Mrs. Stilson's voice

(VOICE live or on tape,
altered or unadorned)

*Oh my God oh my God oh
my God—*

*—trees clouds houses
mostly planes flashing past,
images without words, utter
disarray disbelief, never seen
this kind of thing before!*

*Where am I? How'd I get
here?*

*My leg (What's my leg?)
feels wet arms . . . wet too,
belly same chin nose
everything (Where are they
taking me?) something sticky
(What has happened to my
plane?) feel something
sticky.*

Doors! Too many doors!

*Must have . . . fallen cannot
. . . move at all sky . . .
(Gliding!) dark cannot . . .
talk (Feel as if I'm gliding!).*

*Yes, feels cool, nice . . .
Yes, this is the life all right!*

Images	Sounds outside herself

In this vast whiteness, like apparitions, partial glimpses of doctors and nurses can be seen. They appear and disappear like a pulse. They are never in one place for long. The mirrors multiply their incomprehensibility.

Of random crowd noises, the crowd greatly agitated. In the crowd, people can be heard calling for help, a doctor, an ambulance. But all the sounds are garbled.

Of people whispering.

Of many people asking questions simultaneously, no question comprehensible.

Sometimes the dark panels are opaque, sometimes transparent. Always, they convey a sense of layers, multiplicity, separation. Sense constantly of doors opening, closing, opening, closing.

Of doors opening, closing, opening, closing.

Of someone breathing oxygen through a mask.

VOICES (garbled): Just relax. / No one's going to hurt you. / Can you hear us? / Be careful! / You're hurting her! / No, we're not. / Don't lift her, leave her where she is! / Someone call an ambulance! / I don't think she can hear.

Fragments of hospital equipment appear out of nowhere and disappear just as suddenly. Glimpse always too brief to enable us to identify what this equipment is, or what its purpose.

MALE VOICE: Have you any idea—

OTHER VOICES (garbled): Do you know your name? / Do you know where you are? / What year is this? / If I say the tiger has been killed by the lion, which animal is dead?

Mrs. Stilson's movements seem random. She is a person wandering through space, lost.

A hospital paging system heard.

Mrs. Stilson's voice

*My plane! What has
happened to my plane!*

Help . . .

*—all around faces of which
nothing known no sense
ever all wiped out blank like
ice I think saw it once flying
over something some place
all was white sky and sea
clouds ice almost crashed
couldn't tell where I was
heading right side up
topsy-turvy under over I was
flying actually if I can I do
yes do recall was upside
down can you believe it
almost scraped my head on
the ice caps couldn't tell
which way was up wasn't
even dizzy strange things
happen to me that they do!*

*What's my name? I don't
know my name!*

*Where's my arm? I don't
have an arm!*

What's an arm?

Images	Sounds outside herself
Finally, Mrs. Stilson is led by attendants downstage, to a chair. Then left alone.	Equipment being moved through stone corridors, vast vaulting space. Endless echoing.

Mrs. Stilson's voice

*AB-ABC-ABC123DE451212
what? 123—12345678972357
better yes no problem I'm
okay soon be out soon be
over storm . . . will pass I'm
sure. Always has.*

Awakening

In performance, the end of the Catastrophe section should blend, without interruption, into the beginning of this.

MRS. STILSON DOWNSTAGE ON A CHAIR IN A POOL OF
LIGHT, DARKNESS ALL AROUND HER. IN THE DISTANCE
BEHIND HER, MUFFLED SOUNDS OF A HOSPITAL.
VAGUE IMAGES OF DOCTORS, NURSES ATTENDING TO
SOMEONE WE CANNOT SEE. ONE OF THE DOCTORS
CALLS MRS. STILSON'S NAME. DOWNSTAGE, MRS.
STILSON SHOWS NO TRACE OF RECOGNITION. THE
DOCTOR CALLS HER NAME AGAIN. AGAIN NO
RESPONSE. ONE OF THE DOCTORS SAYS, "IT'S
POSSIBLE SHE MAY HEAR US BUT BE UNABLE TO
RESPOND."

ONE OF THE NURSES TRIES CALLING OUT HER NAME.
STILL NO RESPONSE. THE DOCTOR LEAVES. THE
REMAINING DOCTORS AND NURSES FADE INTO THE
DARKNESS.

ONLY MRS. STILSON CAN BE SEEN.

PAUSE.

MRS. STILSON: *Still . . . sun moon too or . . . three times
happened maybe globbidged rubbidged uff and firded-forded
me to nothing there try again* [WE HEAR A WINDOW BEING
RAISED SOMEWHERE BEHIND HER] *window! up and heard*
[SOUNDS OF BIRDS] *known them know I know them once
upon a birds! that's it better getting better soon be out of
this.*

PAUSE.

Out of . . . what?

PAUSE.

*Dark . . . space vast of . . . in I am or so it seems feels no
real clues to speak of.* [BEHIND HER, BRIEF IMAGE OF A
DOCTOR PASSING] *Something tells me I am not alone.
Once! Lost it. No here back thanks work fast now, yes empty
vast reach of space desert think they call it I'll come back to*

that anyhow down I . . . something what [BRIEF IMAGE OF A NURSE] *it's SOMETHING ELSE IS ENTERING MY!—no wait got it crashing OH MY GOD! CRASHING! deadstick dead-of-night thought the stars were airport lights upside down was I what a way to land glad no one there to see it, anyhow tubbish blaxed and vinkled I commenshed to uh-oh where's it gone to somewhere flubbished what?* with [BRIEF IMAGES OF HOSPITAL STAFF ON THE MOVE] *images are SOMETHING ODD IS! . . . yes, then there I thank you crawling sands and knees still can feel it hear the wind all alone somehow wasn't scared why a mystery, vast dark track of space, we've all got to die that I know, anyhow then day came light came with it so with this you'd think you'd hope just hold on they will find me I am . . . still intact.*

PAUSE.

In here.

LONG SILENCE.

Seem to be the word removed.

LONG SILENCE.

How long have I been here? . . . And wrapped in dark.

PAUSE.

Can remember nothing.

OUTSIDE SOUNDS BEGIN TO IMPINGE; SAME FOR IMAGES. IN THE DISTANCE, AN ATTENDANT DIMLY SEEN PUSHING A FLOOR POLISHER. ITS NOISE RESEMBLES AN ANIMAL'S GROWL.

[TRYING HARD TO BE CHEERY]: *No, definitely I am not alone!*

THE SOUND OF THE POLISHER GROWS LOUDER,

SEEMS MORE BESTIAL, VORACIOUS; IT OVERWHELMS
EVERYTHING. EXPLOSION! SHE GASPS.

[RAPIDLY AND IN PANIC, SENSE OF GREAT COMMOTION
BEHIND HER. A CRISIS HAS OCCURRED] *There I go there
I go hallway now it's screaming crowded pokes me then the
coolbreeze needle scent of sweetness can see palms
flowers flummers couldn't fix the leaking sprouting
everywhere to save me help me CUTS UP THROUGH to
something movement I am something moving without
movement!*

SOUND OF A WOMAN'S MUFFLED SCREAM FROM
BEHIND HER. THE SCREAM GROWS LOUDER.

[WITH DELIGHT] *What a strange adventure I am having!*

LIGHTS TO BLACK ON EVERYTHING.

IN THE DARK, A PAUSE.

WHEN HER VOICE IS HEARD AGAIN, IT IS HEARD FIRST
FROM ALL THE SPEAKERS. HER VOICE SOUNDS
GROGGY, SLURRED. NO LONGER ANY SENSE OF PANIC
DISCERNIBLE. A FEW MOMENTS AFTER HER VOICE IS
HEARD, THE LIGHTS COME UP SLOWLY ON HER. SOON,
ONLY SHE IS SPEAKING; THE VOICE FROM THE
SPEAKERS HAS DISAPPEARED.

*Hapst aporkshop fleetish yes of course it's yes the good ol'
times when we would mollis I mean collis all around still what
my son's name is cannot for the life of me yet face gleams
smiles as he tells them what I did but what his name is
cannot see it pleasant anyway yes palms now ocean sea
breeze wafting floating up and lifting holding weightless and
goes swooooping down with me least I . . . think it's me.*

SOUND OF SOMETHING FLAPPING RAPIDLY OPEN AND
CLOSED, OPEN AND CLOSED.

SOUND OF WIND.

LIGHTS CHANGE INTO A COOL AND AIRY BLUE. SENSE
OF WEIGHTLESSNESS, SERENITY.

IN ANOTHER REALM NOW.

*Yes, out there walking not holding even danger ever-present
how I loved it love it still no doubt will again hear them
cheering wisht or waltz away to some place like Rumania . . .*

THE WIND DISAPPEARS.

Nothing . . .

THE SERENE BLUE LIGHT BEGINS TO FADE AWAY.
SOME PLACE ELSE NOW THAT SHE IS GOING.

*Of course beyond that yet 1, 2 came before the yeast rose
bubbled and MY CHUTE DIDN'T OPEN PROPERLY! Still for
a girl did wonders getting down and it was Charles! no
Charlie, who is Charlie? see him smiling as they tell him
what I—*

OUTSIDE WORLD BEGINS TO IMPINGE. LIGHTS ARE
CHANGING, GROWING BRIGHTER, SOMETHING ODD IS
HAPPENING. SENSE OF IMMINENCE. SHE NOTICES.

[BREATHLESS WITH EXCITEMENT]: *Stop hold cut stop wait
stop come-out-break-out light can see it ready heart can yes
can feel it pounding something underway here light is getting
brighter lids I think the word is that's it lifting of their own but
slowly knew I should be patient should be what? wait hold on
steady now it's spreading no no question something
underway here spreading brighter rising lifting light almost
yes can almost there a little more now yes can almost see
this . . . place I'm . . . in and . . .*

LOOK OF HORROR.

Oh my God! Now I understand! THEY'VE GOT ME!

FOR FIRST TIME DOCTORS, NURSES, HOSPITAL
EQUIPMENT ALL CLEARLY VISIBLE BEHIND HER. ALL
ARE GATHERED AROUND SOMEONE WE CANNOT SEE.
FROM THE WAY THEY ARE ALL BENDING OVER, WE
SURMISE THIS PERSON WE CANNOT SEE IS LYING IN A
BED.

LIGHTS DROP ON MRS. STILSON, DOWNSTAGE.

NURSE [TALKING TO THE PERSON UPSTAGE WE
CANNOT SEE]: Mrs. Stilson, can you open up your eyes?

PAUSE.

MRS. STILSON [SEPARATED FROM HER QUESTIONERS
BY GREAT DISTANCE]: *Don't know how.*

DOCTOR: Mrs. Stilson, you just opened up your eyes. We
saw you. Can you open them again?

NO RESPONSE.

Mrs. Stilson . . .?

MRS. STILSON [PROUDLY, TRIUMPHANTLY]: *My name
then—Mrs. Stilson!*

VOICE ON P.A. SYSTEM: Mrs. Howard, call on three! Mrs.
Howard . . . !

MRS. STILSON: *My name then—Mrs. Howard?*

LIGHTS FADE TO BLACK ON HOSPITAL STAFF.

SOUND OF WIND, SENSE OF TIME PASSING.

LIGHTS COME UP ON MRS. STILSON. THE WIND
DISAPPEARS.

The room that I am in is large, square. What does large mean?

PAUSE.

The way I'm turned I can see a window. When I'm on my back the window isn't there.

DOCTOR [IN THE DISTANCE, AT BEST ONLY DIMLY SEEN]: Mrs. Stilson, can you hear me?

MRS. STILSON: *Yes.*

SECOND DOCTOR: Mrs. Stilson, can you hear me?

MRS. STILSON: *Yes! I said yes! What's wrong with you?*

FIRST DOCTOR: Mrs. Stilson, CAN YOU HEAR ME!

MRS. STILSON: *Don't believe this—I've been put in with the deaf!*

SECOND DOCTOR: Mrs. Stilson, if you can hear us, nod your head.

MRS. STILSON: *All right, fine, that's how you want to play it —there!*

SHE NODS.

THE DOCTORS EXCHANGE GLANCES.

FIRST DOCTOR: Mrs. Stilson, if you can hear us, NOD YOUR HEAD!

MRS. STILSON: *Oh my God, this is grotesque!*

CACOPHONY OF SOUNDS HEARD FROM ALL AROUND, BOTH LIVE AND FROM THE SPEAKERS. IMAGES SUGGESTING SENSATION OF ASSAULT AS WELL.

IMPLICATION OF ALL THESE SOUNDS AND IMAGES IS
THAT MRS. STILSON IS BEING MOVED THROUGH THE
HOSPITAL FOR PURPOSES OF EXAMINATION, PERHAPS
EVEN TORTURE. THE INFORMATION WE RECEIVE
COMES IN TOO FAST AND DISTORTED FOR RATIONAL
COMPREHENSION. THE REALM SHE IS IN IS
TERRIFYING. FORTUNATELY, SHE IS NOT IN IT LONG.

AS LONG AS SHE IS, HOWEVER, THE SENSE SHOULD
BE CONVEYED THAT HER WORLD MOVES AROUND HER
MORE THAN SHE THROUGH IT.

WHAT WE HEAR (THE COMPONENTS): Are we moving you
too fast? / Mustlian pottid or blastigrate, no not that way
this, that's fletchit gottit careful now. / Now put your nose
here on this line, would you? That's it, thank you, well done,
well done. / How are the wickets today? / [SOUND OF
A COUGH] / Now close your— / Is my finger going up
or— / Can you feel this? / Can you feel this? / Name
something that grows on trees. / Who fixes teeth? /
What room do you cook in? / What year is this? / How
long have you been here? / Are we being too rippled
shotgun? / Would you like a cup of tea? / What is Jim
short for? / Point to your shoulder. / No, your shoulder.
/ What do you do with a book? / Don't worry, the water's
warm. We're holding you, don't worry. In we go, that's a girl!

AND THEN, AS SUDDENLY AS THE ASSAULT BEGAN, IT
IS OVER.

ONCE AGAIN, MRS. STILSON ALL ALONE ON STAGE,
DARKNESS ALL AROUND HER, NO SENSE OF WALLS OR
FURNITURE. UTTER ISOLATION.

MRS. STILSON [TRYING HARD TO KEEP SMILING]: *Yes,
all in all I'd say while things could be better could be worse,
far worse, how? Not quite sure. Just a sense I have. The sort
of sense that only great experience can mallees or rake,
plake I mean, flake . . . Drake! That's it.*

SHE STARES INTO SPACE.

SILENCE.

IN THE DISTANCE BEHIND HER, TWO DOCTORS
APPEAR.

FIRST DOCTOR: Mrs. Stilson, who was the first President of
the United States?

MRS. STILSON: *Washington.*

PAUSE.

SECOND DOCTOR [SPEAKING MORE SLOWLY THAN THE
FIRST DOCTOR DID; PERHAPS SHE SIMPLY DIDN'T HEAR
THE QUESTION]: Mrs. Stilson, who was the first President of
the United States?

MRS. STILSON: *Washington!*

SECOND DOCTOR [TO FIRST]: I don't think she hears
herself.

FIRST DOCTOR: No, I don't think she hears herself.

THE TWO DOCTORS EMERGE FROM THE SHADOWS,
APPROACH MRS. STILSON. SHE LOOKS UP IN TERROR.
THIS SHOULD BE THE FIRST TIME THAT THE WOMAN
ON STAGE HAS BEEN DIRECTLY FACED OR
CONFRONTED BY THE HOSPITAL STAFF. HER INNER
AND OUTER WORLDS ARE BEGINNING TO COME
TOGETHER.

FIRST DOCTOR: Mrs. Stilson, makey your naming powers?

MRS. STILSON: What?

SECOND DOCTOR: Canju spokeme?

MRS. STILSON: Can I what?

FIRST DOCTOR: Can do peeperear?

MRS. STILSON: *Don't believe what's going on!*

SECOND DOCTOR: Ahwill.

FIRST DOCTOR: Pollycadjis.

SECOND DOCTOR: Sewyladda?

FIRST DOCTOR [WITH A NOD]: Hm-hm.

EXIT DOCTORS.

MRS. STILSON [ALONE AGAIN]: *How it came to pass that I was captured!* [SHE PONDERS] *Hard to say really. I'll come back to that.*

PAUSE.

The room that I've been put in this time is quite small, square, what does square mean? . . . Means . . .

SENSE OF TIME PASSING. THE LIGHTS SHIFT. THE SPACE SHE IS IN BEGINS TO CHANGE ITS SHAPE.

Of course morning comes I think . . . [SHE PONDERS] *Yes, and night of course comes . . .* [PONDERS MORE] *Though sometimes . . .*

MRS. STILSON SOME PLACE ELSE NOW. AND SHE IS AWARE OF IT.

Yes, the way the walls choose to move around me . . . Yes, I've noticed that, I'm no fool!

A NURSE APPEARS CARRYING A DAZZLING BOUQUET OF FLOWERS. THIS BOUQUET IS THE FIRST REAL

COLOR WE HAVE SEEN.

NURSE: Good morning! Look what somebody's just sent you!
[SHE SETS THEM ON A TABLE] Wish I had as many
admirers as you.

EXIT NURSE, SMILING WARMLY.

MRS. STILSON'S EYES ARE DRAWN TO THE FLOWERS.
AND SOMETHING ABOUT THEM APPARENTLY RENDERS
IT IMPOSSIBLE FOR HER TO SHIFT HER GAZE AWAY.
SOMETHING ABOUT THESE FLOWERS HAS HER IN
THEIR THRALL.

WHAT IT IS IS THEIR COLOR.

IT IS AS IF SHE HAS NEVER EXPERIENCED COLOR
BEFORE. AND THE EXPERIENCE IS SO OVERWHELMING,
BOTH PHYSIOLOGICALLY AND PSYCHOLOGICALLY,
THAT HER BRAIN CANNOT PROCESS ALL THE
INFORMATION. HER CIRCUITRY IS OVERLOADED. IT IS
TOO MUCH SENSORY INPUT FOR HER TO HANDLE. AN
EXPLOSION IS IMMINENT. IF SOMETHING DOES NOT
INTERVENE TO DIVERT HER ATTENTION, MRS. STILSON
WILL VERY LIKELY FAINT, PERHAPS EVEN SUFFER A
SEIZURE.

A NARROW BEAM OF LIGHT, GROWING STEADILY IN
INTENSITY, FALLS UPON THE BOUQUET OF FLOWERS,
CAUSING THEIR COLORS TO TAKE ON AN INTENSITY
THEMSELVES THAT THEY OTHERWISE WOULD LACK. AT
THE SAME TIME, A SINGLE MUSICAL TONE IS HEARD,
VOLUME INCREASING.

A NURSE ENTERS THE ROOM.

NURSE: May I get you something?

MRS. STILSON [ABSTRACTED, EYES REMAINING ON THE
FLOWERS]: Yes, a sweater.

NURSE: Yes, of course. Think we have one here. [THE NURSE OPENS A DRAWER, TAKES OUT A PILLOW, HANDS THE PILLOW TO MRS. STILSON] Here.

MRS. STILSON ACCEPTS THE PILLOW UNQUESTIONINGLY, EYES NEVER LEAVING THE FLOWERS. SHE LAYS THE PILLOW ON HER LAP, PROMPTLY FORGETS ABOUT IT. THE MUSICAL TONE AND THE BEAM OF LIGHT CONTINUE RELENTLESSLY TOWARD THEIR PEAK.

THE NURSE, OBLIVIOUS OF ANY CRISIS, EXITS.

THE SINGLE TONE AND THE BEAM OF LIGHT CREST TOGETHER.

SILENCE FOLLOWS. THE BEAM DISAPPEARS. THE FLOWERS SEEM NORMAL. THE LIGHTS AROUND MRS. STILSON RETURN TO THE WAY THEY WERE BEFORE THE GIFT OF FLOWERS WAS BROUGHT IN.

MRS. STILSON [SHAKEN]: *This is not a hospital of course, and I know it! What it is is a farmhouse made up to look like a hospital. Why? I'll come back to that.*

ENTER ANOTHER NURSE.

NURSE: Hi! Haven't seen you in a while. Have you missed me?

MRS. STILSON [NO HINT OF RECOGNITION VISIBLE]: What?

NURSE [WARMLY]: They say you didn't touch your dinner. Would you like some pudding?

MRS. STILSON: No.

NURSE: Good, I'll go get you some.

EXIT NURSE, VERY CHEERFULLY.

MRS. STILSON: *Yes no question they have got me I've been what that word was captured is it? No it's—Yes, it's captured how? Near as it can figure. I was in my prane and crashed, not unusual, still in all not too common. Neither is it very grub. Plexit rather or I'd say propopic. Well that's that, jungdaball! Anyhow to resume, what I had for lunch? That's not it, good books I have read, good what, done what? Whaaaaat? Do the busy here! Get inside this, rubbidge all around let the vontul do some yes off or it of above semilacrum pwooosh! what with noddygobbit nip-n-crashing inside outside witsit watchit funnel vortex sucking into backlash watchit get-out caught-in spinning ring-grab grobbit help woooosh! cannot stoppit on its own has me where it wants* [AND SUDDENLY SHE IS IN ANOTHER REALM. LIGHTS TRANSFORMED INTO WEIGHTLESS BLUE. SENSE OF EASE AND SERENITY] *Plane! See it thanks, okay, onto back we were and here it is. Slow down easy now. Captured. After crashing, that is what we said or was about to, think it so, cannot tell for sure, s l o w   i t   s l o w   i t, okay here we go . . .* [SPEAKING SLOWER NOW] *captured after crashing by the enemy and brought here to this farm masquerading as a hospital. Why? For I would say offhand information. Of what sort though hard to tell. For example, questions such as can I raise my fingers, what's an overcoat, how many nickels in a rhyme, questions such as these. To what use can they be to the enemy? Hard to tell from here. Nonetheless, I would say must be certain information I possess that they want well I won't give it I'll escape! Strange things happen to me that they do! Good thing I'm all right! Must be in Rumania. Just a hunch of course.* [THE SERENE BLUE LIGHT STARTS TO FADE] *Ssssh, someone's coming.*

A NURSE HAS ENTERED. THE NURSE GUIDES MRS. STILSON TO A DOCTOR. THE BLUE LIGHT IS GONE. THE NURSE LEAVES.

THE SPACE MRS. STILSON NOW IS IN APPEARS MUCH

MORE "REAL" AND LESS FRAGMENTARY THAN WHAT
WE HAVE SO FAR BEEN OBSERVING. WE SEE MRS.
STILSON HERE AS OTHERS SEE HER.

DOCTOR: Mrs. Stilson, if you don't mind, I'd like to ask you
some questions. Some will be easy, some will be hard. Is
that all right?

MRS. STILSON: Oh yes I'd say oh well yes that's the twither
of it.

DOCTOR: Good. Okay. Where were you born?

MRS. STILSON: Never. Not at all. Here the match wundles
up you know and drats flames fires I keep careful always—

DOCTOR: Right . . . [SPEAKING VERY SLOWLY, PRECISE
ENUNCIATION] Where were you born?

MRS. STILSON: Well now well now that's a good thing
knowing yushof course wouldn't call it such as I did
andinjurations or aplovia could it? No I wouldn't think so.
Next?

PAUSE.

DOCTOR: Mrs. Stilson, are there seven days in a week?

MRS. STILSON: . . . Seven . . . Yes.

DOCTOR: Are there five days in a week?

PAUSE.

MRS. STILSON [AFTER MUCH PONDERING]: No.

DOCTOR: Can a stone float on water?

LONG PAUSE.

MRS. STILSON: No.

DOCTOR: Mrs. Stilson, can you cough?

MRS. STILSON: Somewhat.

DOCTOR: Well, would you show me how you cough?

MRS. STILSON: Well now well now not so easy what you cromplie is to put these bushes open and—

DOCTOR: No no, Mrs. Stilson, I'm sorry—I would like to hear you cough.

MRS. STILSON: Well I'm not bort you know with plajits or we'd see it wencherday she brings its pillow with the fistils-opening I'd say outward always outward never stopping it.

LONG SILENCE.

DOCTOR: Mrs. Stilson, I have some objects here. [HE TAKES A COMB, A TOOTHBRUSH, A PACK OF MATCHES, AND A KEY FROM HIS POCKET, SETS THEM DOWN WHERE SHE CAN SEE] Could you point to the object you would use for cleaning your teeth?

VERY LONG SILENCE.

FINALLY SHE PICKS UP THE COMB AND SHOWS IT TO HIM. THEN SHE PUTS IT DOWN. WAITS.

Mrs. Stilson, here, take this object in your hand. [HE HANDS HER THE TOOTHBRUSH] Do you know what this object is called?

MRS. STILSON [WITH GREAT DIFFICULTY]: Tooooooooovvvv . . . bbbrum?

DOCTOR: Very good. Now put it down.

SHE PUTS IT DOWN.

Now, pretend you have it in your hand. Show me what you'd do with it.

SHE DOES NOTHING.

What does one do with an object such as that, Mrs. Stilson?

NO RESPONSE.

Mrs. Stilson, what is the name of the object you are looking at?

MRS. STILSON: Well it's . . . wombly and not at all . . . rigged or tuned like we might twunter or toring to work the clambness out of it or—

DOCTOR: Pick it up.

MRS. STILSON [AS SOON AS SHE'S PICKED IT UP]: Tooovebram, tooove-britch bratch brush bridge, two-bridge.

DOCTOR: Show me what you do with it.

FOR SEVERAL MOMENTS SHE DOES NOTHING.

THEN SHE PUTS IT TO HER LIPS, HOLDS IT THERE MOTIONLESS.

Very good. Thank you.

SHE SIGHS HEAVILY, PUTS IT DOWN.

THE DOCTOR GATHERS UP HIS OBJECTS, LEAVES.

ONCE AGAIN MRS. STILSON ALL ALONE.

SHE STARES INTO SPACE.

THEN HER VOICE IS HEARD COMING FROM ALL
AROUND; SHE HERSELF DOES NOT SPEAK.

HER VOICE: *Dark now again out the window on my side
lying here all alone . . .*

VERY LONG SILENCE.

MRS. STILSON: *Yesterday my children came to see me.*

PAUSE.

*Or at least, I was told they were my children. Never saw
them before in my life.*

SHE STARES OUT, MOTIONLESS. NO EXPRESSION.

THEN AFTER A WHILE SHE LOOKS AROUND. STUDIES
THE DARK FOR CLUES.

Time has become peculiar.

AND SHE CONTINUES THIS SCRUTINY OF THE DARK.

BUT IF THIS ACTIVITY STEMS FROM CURIOSITY, IT IS A
MILD CURIOSITY AT MOST. NO LONGER DOES SHE
CONVEY OR PROBABLY EVEN EXPERIENCE THE
EXTREME, DISORIENTED DREAD WE SAW EARLIER
WHEN SHE FIRST ARRIVED IN THIS NEW REALM. HER
SENSE OF URGENCY IS GONE. INDEED, WERE WE ABLE
TO OBSERVE MRS. STILSON CONSTANTLY, WE WOULD
INEVITABLY CONCLUDE THAT HER CURIOSITY IS NOW
ONLY MINIMALLY PURPOSEFUL; THAT, IN FACT, MORE
LIKELY HER INVESTIGATIONS ARE THE ACTIONS,
POSSIBLY MERELY THE REFLEX ACTIONS, OF SOMEONE
WITH LITTLE OR NOTHING ELSE TO DO.

THIS IS NOT TO DENY THAT SHE IS DESPERATELY
TRYING TO PIECE HER SHATTERED WORLD TOGETHER.
UNDOUBTEDLY, IT IS THE DOMINANT MOTIF IN HER

MIND. BUT IT IS A MOTIF PROBABLY MORE ABSENT
FROM HER CONSCIOUSNESS THAN PRESENT, AND THE
QUEST IT INSPIRES IS INTERMITTENT AT BEST. HER
MENTAL ABILITIES HAVE NOT ONLY BEEN SEVERELY
ALTERED, THEY HAVE BEEN DIMINISHED: THAT IS THE
TERRIBLE FACT ONE CANNOT DENY.

AND THEN SUDDENLY SHE IS AGITATED.

Mother! . . . didn't say as she usually . . .

PAUSE.

*And I thought late enough or early rather first light coming so
when didn't move I poked her then with shoving but she
didn't even eyes or giggle when I tickled.*

PAUSE.

What it was was not a trick as I at first had—

PAUSE.

*Well I couldn't figure, he had never lied, tried to get her hold
me couldn't it was useless. Then his face was, I had never
known a face could . . . It was like a mask then like sirens it
was bursting open it was him then I too joining it was
useless. Can still feel what it was like when she held me.*

PAUSE.

*So then well I was on my own. He was all destroyed, had I
think they say no strength for this.*

THEN SHE'S SILENT. NO EXPRESSION. STARES INTO
SPACE.

ENTER A DOCTOR AND A NURSE.

DOCTOR [WARMLY]: Hello, Mrs. Stilson.

HE COMES OVER NEXT TO HER. WE CANNOT TELL IF
SHE NOTICES HIM OR NOT. THE NURSE, CHART IN
HAND, STANDS A SLIGHT DISTANCE AWAY.

You're looking much, much better. [HE SMILES AND SITS
DOWN NEXT TO HER. HE WATCHES HER FOR SEVERAL
MOMENTS, SEARCHING FOR SIGNS OF RECOGNITION]
Mrs. Stilson, do you know why you're here?

MRS. STILSON: Well now well now . . .

SHE GIVES IT UP.

SILENCE.

DOCTOR: You have had an accident—

MRS. STILSON:
[HER WORDS
OVERPOWERING HIS]

*I don't trust him, don't trust
anyone. Must get word out,
send a message where I am.
Like a wall between me and
others. No one ever gets it
right even though I tell them
right. They are playing tricks
on me, two sides, both not
my friends, goes in goes out
too fast too fast hurts do the
busy I'm all right I talk right
why acting all these others
like I don't, what's he
marking, what's he writing?*

DOCTOR:
[TO ALL INTENTS AND
PURPOSES, WHAT HE
SAYS IS LOST]
At home. Not in an airplane.
It's called a stroke. This
means that your brain has
been injured and brain tissue
destroyed, though we are
not certain of the cause. You
could get better, and you're
certainly making progress.
But it's still too soon to give
any sort of exact prognosis.
[HE STUDIES HER. THEN
HE RISES AND MARKS
SOMETHING ON HIS
CLIPBOARD]

EXIT DOCTOR AND NURSE.

MRS. STILSON: *I am doing well of course!*

PAUSE.

[SECRETIVE TONE] *They still pretend they do not understand me. I believe they may be mad.*

PAUSE.

No they're not mad, I am mad. Today I heard it. Everything I speak is wronged. SOMETHING HAS BEEN DONE TO ME!

DOCTOR [BARELY VISIBLE IN THE DISTANCE]: Mrs. Stilson, can you repeat this phrase: "We live across the street from the school."

SHE PONDERS.

MRS. STILSON: "Malacats on the forturay are the kesterfats of the romancers."

LOOK OF HORROR COMES ACROSS HER FACE; THE DOCTOR VANISHES.

THROUGH THE SCREENS, UPSTAGE, WE SEE A NURSE BRINGING ON A TRAY OF FOOD.

NURSE [BRIGHTLY]: Okay ups-a-girl, ups-a-baby, dinnertime! Open wide now, mustn't go dribble-dribble—at's-a-way!

MRS. STILSON SCREAMS, SWINGS HER ARMS IN FURY. IN THE DISTANCE, UPSTAGE, THE TRAY OF FOOD GOES FLYING.

MRS. STILSON [SCREAMING]: Out! Get out! Take this shit away, I don't want it! Someone get me out of here!

NURSE [WHILE MRS. STILSON CONTINUES SHOUTING]: Help, someone, come quick! She's talking! Good as you or me! It's a miracle! Help! Somebody! Come quick!

WHILE MRS. STILSON CONTINUES TO SCREAM AND

FLAIL HER ARMS, NURSES AND DOCTORS RUSH ON
UPSTAGE AND SURROUND THE PATIENT WE NEVER
SEE.

AND ALTHOUGH MRS. STILSON CONTINUES TO SCREAM
COHERENTLY, IN FACT SHE ISN'T ANY BETTER, NO
MIRACLE HAS OCCURRED. HER ABILITY TO ARTICULATE
WITH APPARENT NORMALCY HAS BEEN BROUGHT ON
BY EXTREME AGITATION AND IN NO WAY IMPLIES THAT
SHE COULD PRODUCE THESE SOUNDS AGAIN "IF SHE
ONLY WANTED"; WILL POWER HAS NOTHING TO DO
WITH WHAT WE HEAR.

HER LANGUAGE, AS IT MUST, SOON SLIPS BACK INTO
JARGON. SHE CONTINUES TO FLAIL HER ARMS. IN THE
BACKGROUND, WE CAN SEE A NURSE PREPARING A
HYPODERMIC.

MRS. STILSON [STRUGGLING]:—flubdgy please
no-mommy-callming holdmeplease to sleeEEEEP SHOOOOP
shop shnoper CRROOOOOCK SNANNNNG wuduitcoldly
should I gobbin flutter truly HELP ME yessisnofun, snofun,
wishes awhin dahd killminsilf if . . . could [IN THE
DISTANCE, WE SEE THE NEEDLE GIVEN] OW! . . . would I
but . . . [SHE'S BECOMING DROWSY] . . . awful to me him
as well moas of all no cantduit . . . jusscantduit . . .

HEAD DROPS.

INTO SLEEP SHE GOES.

EXIT DOCTORS, NURSES.

SOUND OF A GENTLE WIND IS HEARD.

LIGHTS FADE TO BLACK ON MRS. STILSON.

DARKNESS EVERYWHERE; THE SOUND OF THE WIND
FADES AWAY.

SILENCE.

LIGHTS UP ON AMY, DOWNSTAGE RIGHT.

THEN LIGHTS UP ON MRS. STILSON STARING INTO SPACE.

AMY: Mrs. Stilson?

MRS. STILSON TURNS TOWARD THE SOUND, SEES AMY.

You have had what's called a stroke.

CHANGE OF LIGHTS AND PANELS OPEN. SENSE OF TERRIBLE ENCLOSURE GONE. BIRDS HEARD. WE ARE OUTSIDE NOW. AMY PUTS A SHAWL AROUND MRS. STILSON'S SHOULDERS.

AMY: Are you sure that will be enough?

MRS. STILSON: Oh yes . . . thhhankyou.

SHE TUCKS THE SHAWL AROUND HERSELF.

THEN AMY GUIDES HER THROUGH THE PANELS AS IF THROUGH CORRIDORS; NO RUSH, SLOW GENTLE STROLL.

THEY EMERGE OTHER SIDE OF STAGE. WARM LIGHT. AMY TAKES IN THE VIEW. MRS. STILSON APPEARS INDIFFERENT.

AMY: Nice to be outside, isn't it? . . . Nice view.

MRS. STILSON [STILL WITH INDIFFERENCE]: Yes indeed.

THERE ARE TWO CHAIRS NEARBY, AND THEY SIT.

SILENCE FOR A TIME.

AMY: Are you feeling any better today?

BUT SHE GETS NO RESPONSE.

THEN, A MOMENT LATER, MRS. STILSON TURNS TO
AMY; IT IS AS IF AMY'S QUESTION HAS NOT EVEN BEEN
HEARD.

MRS. STILSON: The thing is . . .

BUT THE STATEMENT TRAILS OFF INTO NOTHINGNESS.

SHE STARES OUT, NO EXPRESSION.

AMY: Yes? What?

LONG SILENCE.

MRS. STILSON: I can't make it do it like it used to.

AMY: Yes, I know. That's because of the accident.

MRS. STILSON [SEEMINGLY OBLIVIOUS OF AMY'S
WORDS]: The words, they go in somelimes then out they go,
I can't stop them here inside or make maybe globbidge to
the tubberway or—

AMY: Emily. Emily!

MRS. STILSON [SHAKEN OUT OF HERSELF]: . . . What?

AMY: Did you hear what you just said?

MRS. STILSON: . . . Why?

AMY [SPEAKING SLOWLY]: You must listen to what you're
saying.

MRS. STILSON: Did I . . . do . . .

AMY [NODDING, SMILING; CLEARLY NO REPROACH INTENDED]: Slow down. Listen to what you're saying.

SILENCE.

MRS. STILSON [SLOWER]: The thing is . . . doing all this busy in here gets, you know with the talking it's like . . . sometimes when I hear here [SHE TOUCHES HER HEAD] . . . but when I start to . . . kind more what kind of voice should . . . it's like pfffft! [SHE MAKES A GESTURE WITH HER HAND OF SOMETHING FLYING AWAY]

AMY [SMILING]: Yes, I know. It's hard to find the words for what you're thinking of.

MRS. STILSON: Well yes.

LONG PAUSE.

And then these people, they keep waiting . . . And I see they're smiling and . . . they keep . . . waiting . . .[FAINT SMILE, HELPLESS GESTURE. SHE STARES OFF]

LONG SILENCE.

AMY: Emily.

MRS. STILSON LOOKS UP.

Can you remember anything about your life . . . before the accident?

MRS. STILSON: Not sometimes, some days it goes better if I see a thing or smell . . . it . . . remembers me back, you see? And I see things that maybe they were me and maybe they were just some things you know that happens in the night when you . . . [STRUGGLING VISIBLY] have your things closed, eyes.

AMY: A dream you mean.

MRS. STILSON [WITH RELIEF]: Yes. So I don't know for sure.

PAUSE.

If it was really me.

LONG SILENCE.

AMY: Your son is bringing a picture of you when you were younger. We thought you might like that.

NO VISIBLE RESPONSE. LONG SILENCE.

You used to fly, didn't you?

MRS. STILSON [BRIGHTLY]: Oh yes indeed! Very much! I walked . . . out . . .

PAUSE.

[SOFTLY, PROUDLY] I walked out on wings.

LIGHTS FADE ON AMY. MRS. STILSON ALONE AGAIN.

Sitting here on my bed I can close my eyes shut out all that I can't do with, hearing my own talking, others, names that used to well just be there when I wanted now all somewhere else. No control. Close my eyes then, go to—

SOUND OF SOMETHING FLAPPING RAPIDLY.

A FIBRILLATION.

LIGHTS BECOME BLUE. SENSE OF WEIGHTLESSNESS, SERENITY.

Here I go. No one talks here. Images coming I seem feel it feels better this way here is how it goes: this time I am still in the middle Stilson in the middle going out walking out wind feels good hold the wires feel the hum down below far there

*they are now we turn it bank it now we spin! Looks more bad
than really is, still needs good balance and those nerves and
that thing that courage thing don't fall off! . . . And now I'm
out . . . and back and . . .* [WITH SURPRISE] *there's the
window.*

LIGHTS HAVE RETURNED TO NORMAL. SHE IS BACK
WHERE SHE STARTED.

AMY ENTERS.

AMY: Hello, Emily.

MRS. STILSON: Oh, Amy! . . . Didn't hear what you was . . .
coming here to . . . Oh!

AMY: What is it?

MRS. STILSON: Something . . . wet.

AMY: Do you know what it is?

MRS. STILSON: Don't . . . can't say find it word.

AMY: Try. You can find it.

MRS. STILSON: Wet . . . thing, many, both sides yes.

AMY: Can you name them? What they are? You do know
what they are.

PAUSE.

MRS. STILSON: . . . Tears?

AMY: That's right, very good. Those are tears. And do you
know what that means?

MRS. STILSON: . . . Sad?

AMY: Yes, right, well done, it means . . . that you are sad.

Explorations

STAGE DARK.

IN THE DARK, A PIANO HEARD: SOMEONE FOOLING
AROUND ON THE KEYBOARD, BRIEF HALTING
SNATCHES OF OLD SONGS EMERGING AS THE
PRODUCT; WOULD CONSTITUTE A MEDLEY WERE THE
SEGMENTS ONLY LONGER, MORE COHESIVE. AS IT IS,
SUSPICION AROUSED THAT WHAT WE HEAR IS ALL THE
PIANIST CAN REMEMBER.

SOUND OF GENERAL LAUGHTER, HUBBUB.

LIGHTS RISE.

WHAT WE SEE IS A REC ROOM, IN SOME PLACES
CLEARLY, IN OTHERS NOT (THE ROOM BEING
OBSERVED PARTLY THROUGH THE DARK SCRIM
PANELS).

UPSTAGE RIGHT, AN UPRIGHT PIANO, PLAYERS AND
FRIENDS GATHERED ROUND. DOCTORS, THERAPISTS,
NURSES, ATTENDANTS, PATIENTS, VISITORS CERTAINLY
ARE NOT ALL SEEN, BUT THOSE WE DO SEE COME
FROM SUCH A GROUP. WE ARE IN THE REC ROOM OF
A REHABILITATION CENTER. SOME PATIENTS IN
WHEELCHAIRS.

THE ROOM ITSELF HAS BRIGHT COMFORTABLE CHAIRS,
PERHAPS A CARD TABLE, MAGAZINE RACK, CERTAINLY
A TV SET. SOMEONE NOW TURNS ON THE TV.

WHAT EMERGES IS THE SOUND OF ELLA FITZGERALD
IN LIVE PERFORMANCE. SHE SINGS SCAT: MELLOW,
UPBEAT.

THE PATIENTS AND STAFF PERSUADE THE PIANIST TO
CEASE. ELLA'S RIFFS OF SCAT CAST SOMETHING LIKE
A SPELL.

MRS. STILSON WANDERS THROUGH THE SPACE.

THE REC ROOM, IT SHOULD BE STRESSED, SHOWS
MORE DETAIL AND COLOR THAN ANY SPACE WE'VE SO
FAR SEEN. PERHAPS A VASE OF FLOWERS HELPS TO
SIGNAL THAT MRS. STILSON'S WORLD IS BECOMING
FULLER, MORE INTEGRATED.

MOVEMENTS TOO SEEM NORMAL, SAME FOR
CONVERSATIONS THAT GO ON DURING ALL OF THIS,
THOUGH TOO SOFTLY FOR US TO COMPREHEND.

THE MUSIC OF COURSE SETS THE TONE. ALL WHO
LISTEN ARE IN ITS THRALL.

NEW TIME SENSE HERE, A LANGUOR ALMOST. THE
DREAD MRS. STILSON FELT HAS BEEN REPLACED BY
AN ACKNOWLEDGMENT OF HER CONDITION, THOUGH
NOT AN UNDERSTANDING.

IN THIS TIME BEFORE SHE SPEAKS, AND IN FACT
DURING, WE OBSERVE THE LIFE OF THE REC ROOM
BEHIND AND AROUND HER. THIS IS NOT A HOSPITAL
ANY MORE, AND A KIND OF NORMALCY PREVAILS.

THE SENSE SHOULD BE CONVEYED OF CORRIDORS
LEADING TO AND FROM THIS ROOM.

THEN THE MUSIC AND THE REC ROOM SOUNDS GROW
DIM; MRS. STILSON COMES FORWARD, LOST IN THE
DRIFTS OF A THOUGHT.

MRS. STILSON [RELAXED, MELLOW]: *Wonder . . . what's
inside of it . . .?*

PAUSE.

*I mean, how does it work? What's inside that . . . makes it
work?*

LONG PAUSE. SHE PONDERS.

I mean when you . . . think about it all . . .

PAUSE.

*And when you think that it could . . . ever have been . . .
possible to . . . be another way . . .*

SHE PONDERS.

BUT IT'S HARD FOR HER TO KEEP IN MIND WHAT SHE'S
BEEN THINKING OF, AND SHE HAS TO FIGHT THE NOISE
OF THE REC ROOM, ITS INTRUSIVE PRESENCE. LIKE A
NOVICE JUGGLER, MRS. STILSON IS UNABLE TO KEEP
OUTSIDE IMAGES AND INNER THOUGHTS GOING
SIMULTANEOUSLY. WHEN SHE'S WITH HER THOUGHTS,
THE OUTSIDE WORLD FADES AWAY. WHEN THE
OUTSIDE WORLD IS WITH HER, HER THOUGHTS FADE
AWAY.

BUT SHE FIGHTS HER WAY THROUGH IT, AND KEEPS
THE THOUGHT IN MIND.

THE REC ROOM, WHOSE NOISE HAS JUST INCREASED,
GROWS QUIET.

Maybe . . . if somehow I could— [SHE SEARCHES FOR
THE WORDS THAT MATCH HER CONCEPT]*—get inside . . .*

PAUSE.

SOUNDS OF THE REC ROOM PULSE LOUDER. SHE
FIGHTS AGAINST IT. THE REC ROOM SOUNDS DIMINISH.

Prob'ly . . . very dark inside . . . [SHE PONDERS; TRIES TO
PICTURE WHAT SHE'S THINKING] *Yes . . . twisting kind of
place I bet . . .* [PONDERS MORE] *With lots of . . .* [SHE
SEARCHES FOR THE PROPER WORD; FINDS IT] *. . .
passageways that . . . lead to . . .* [AGAIN, SHE SEARCHES
FOR THE WORD]

THE OUTSIDE WORLD RUSHES IN.

PATIENT IN A WHEELCHAIR [ONLY BARELY AUDIBLE]:
My foot feels sour.

AN ATTENDANT PUTS A LAP RUG OVER THE PATIENT'S
LIMBS. THEN THE REC ROOM, ONCE AGAIN, FADES
AWAY.

MRS. STILSON [FIGHTING ON]: . . . *lead to . . . something
. . . Door! Yes . . . closed off now I . . . guess possib . . . ly
for good I mean . . . forever, what does that mean?* [SHE
PONDERS]

ATTENDANT: Would you like some candy?

MRS. STILSON: No.

ATTENDANT: Billy made it.

MRS. STILSON: No!

THE ATTENDANT MOVES BACK INTO THE SHADOWS.

Where was I? [SHE LOOKS AROUND] *Why can't they just
. . . let me . . . be when I'm . . .*

LIGHTS START TO CHANGE. HER WORLD SUDDENLY IN
FLUX. THE REC ROOM FADES FROM VIEW. SOUNDS OF
BIRDS HEARD, DIMLY AT FIRST.

[AWARE OF THE CHANGE AS IT IS OCCURRING] . . .
okay. Slipping out of . . . it and . . .

MRS. STILSON IN A DIFFERENT PLACE.

Outside now! How . . . did I do that?

AMY [EMERGING FROM THE SHADOWS]: Do you like this
new place better?

MRS. STILSON: Oh well oh well yes, much, all . . . nice flowers here, people seem . . . more like me. Thank you.

AMY MOVES BACK TOWARD THE SHADOWS.

And then I see it happen once again . . .

AMY GONE FROM SIGHT.

Amy kisses me. Puts her—what thing is it, arm! yes, arm, puts her arm around my . . .

PAUSE.

. . . shoulder, turns her head away so I can't . . .

PAUSE.

Well, it knows what she's doing. May not get much better even though I'm here. No, I know that. I know that. No real need for her to . . .

LONG PAUSE.

Then she kisses me again.

PAUSE.

Walks away . . .

PAUSE.

LIGHTS CHANGE AGAIN, WORLD AGAIN IN FLUX. NOISES OF THE BUILDING'S INTERIOR CAN BE HEARD LIKE A BABEL, ONLY FLEETINGLY COHERENT. THE REC ROOM SEEN DISSOLVING.

MRS. STILSON: *Where am I?*

SHE BEGINS TO WANDER THROUGH A MAZE OF

PASSAGEWAYS. THE MIRRORS MULTIPLY HER IMAGE, CREATE A SENSE OF ENDLESSNESS.

[*Note. The following blocks of sound, which accompany her expedition, are meant to blend and overlap in performance and, to that end, can be used in any order and combined in any way desired, except for the last five blocks, numbers 12–16, which must be performed in their given sequence and in a way that is comprehensible. The sounds themselves may be live or pre-recorded; those which are pre-recorded should emanate from all parts of the theater and in no predictable pattern. The effect should be exhilarating and disorienting. An adventure. With terrifying aspects to be sure. But the sense of mystery and adventure must never be so overwhelmed by the terror that it is either lost altogether or submerged to the point of insignificance.*

Mrs. Stilson may be frightened here, but the fear does not prevent her from exploring.

She wanders through the labyrinth of dark panels as if they were so many doors, each door leading into yet another realm.]

BLOCK 1: It was but a few years later that Fritsch and Hitzig stimulated the cortex of a dog with an electric current. Here at last was dramatic and indisputable evidence that—

BLOCK 2: Would you like me to change the channel?

BLOCK 3: . . . presented, I would say, essentially similar conclusions on the behavioral correlates of each cerebral convolution.

BLOCK 4 [BEING THE DEEP MALE VOICE, SPEAKING SLOWLY, ENUNCIATING CAREFULLY, THAT ONE HEARS ON THE SPEECH-THERAPY MACHINE KNOWN AS "THE LANGUAGE MASTER"]: Mother led Bud to the bed.

BLOCK 5: . . . In the laboratory then, through electrical stimulation of neural centers or excisions of areas of the

brain, scientists acquired information about the organization
of mental activities in the monkey, the dog, the cat, and the
rat. The discovery of certain peculiar clinical pictures,
reminiscent of bizarre human syndromes, proved of special
interest.

BLOCK 6: Can you tell me what this object's called?

BLOCK 7: ELLA'S RIFFS OF SCAT, AS IF WE WERE STILL
IN THE REC ROOM AFTER ALL.

BLOCK 8: One has only to glance through the writings of this
period to sense the heightened excitement attendant upon
these discoveries!

BLOCK 9: Possibly some diaschisis, which would of course
help account for the apparent mirroring. And then, of course,
we must not overlook the fact that she's left-handed.

BLOCK 10: Of course, you understand, these theories may
all be wrong! [SOUND OF LAUGHTER FROM AN
AUDIENCE] Any other questions? Yes, over there, in the
corner.

BLOCK 11: Mrs. Stilson, this is Dr. Rogans. Dr. Rogans, this
is Emily Stilson.

BLOCK 12: MALE VOICE: —definite possibility I would say of
a tiny subclinical infarct in Penfield's area. Yes? FEMALE
VOICE: Are you sure there is a Penfield's area? MALE
VOICE: No. [LAUGHTER FROM HIS AUDIENCE] MALE
VOICE AGAIN [ITSELF ON THE VERGE OF LAUGHTER]:
But *something* is wrong with her! [RAUCOUS LAUGHTER
FROM HIS AUDIENCE]

[*Note. Emerging out of the laughter in Block 12, a single
musical TONE. This tone increases in intensity. It should
carry through Block 16 and into Mrs. Stilson's emergence
from the maze of panels, helping to propel her into the realm
and the memory to which this expedition has been leading.*]

BLOCK 13: The controversy, of course, is that some feel it's language without thought, and others, thought without language . . .

BLOCK 14: What it is, of course, is the symbol system. Their symbol system's shot. They can't make analogies.

BLOCK 15: You see, it's all so unpredictable. There are no fixed posts, no clear boundaries. The victim, you could say, has been cut adrift . . .

BLOCK 16: Ah, now you're really flying blind there!

MRS. STILSON EMERGES FROM THE MAZE OF CORRIDORS. SOUND PERHAPS OF WIND, OR BELLS. LIGHTS BLUE, SENSE AGAIN OF WEIGHTLESSNESS, AIRINESS.

MRS. STILSON [IN AWE AND ECSTASY]: *As I see it now, the plane was flying BACKWARDS! Really, wind that strong, didn't know it could be! Yet the sky was clear, not a cloud, crystal blue, gorgeous, angels could've lived in sky like that . . . I think the cyclone must've blown in on the Andes from the sea . . .*

BLUE LIGHT FADES. WIND GONE, BELLS GONE, MUSICAL TONE IS GONE.

[COMING OUT OF IT] *Yes* . . . [SHE LOOKS AROUND; GETS HER BEARINGS] *Yes, no question, this . . . place better.* [AND NOW SHE'S LANDED] *All these people just . . . like me, I guess.*

SHE TAKES IN WHERE SHE IS, SEEMS SLIGHTLY STUNNED TO BE BACK WHERE SHE STARTED. SENSE OF WONDERMENT APPARENT.

AN ATTENDANT APPROACHES.

ATTENDANT: Mrs. Stilson?

MRS. STILSON [STARTLED]: Oh!

ATTENDANT: Sorry to—

MRS. STILSON: Is it . . . ?

ATTENDANT: Yes.

MRS. STILSON: Did I . . . ?

ATTENDANT: No, no need to worry. Here, I'll take you.

THE ATTENDANT GUIDES MRS. STILSON TO A THERAPY ROOM, THOUGH, IN FACT, MORE LIKELY (ON THE STAGE) THE ROOM ASSEMBLES AROUND HER. IN THE ROOM ARE AMY, BILLY (A MAN IN HIS MIDDLE THIRTIES), MRS. TIMMINS (ELDERLY, IN A WHEELCHAIR), AND MR. BROWNSTEIN (ALSO ELDERLY AND IN A WHEELCHAIR).

THE ATTENDANT LEAVES.

AMY: Well! Now that we're all here on this lovely afternoon, I thought that maybe—

BILLY: She looks really good.

AMY: What?

BILLY: This new lady here, can't remember what her name is, no bother, anyhow, she looks really nice all dressed like this, an' I jus' wanna extent a nice welcome here on behalf o' all of us.

THE OTHER PATIENTS MUMBLE THEIR ASSENT.

AMY: Well, that is very nice, Billy, very nice. Can any of the rest of you remember this woman's name?

BILLY: I seen her I think when it is, yesterday, how's that?

AMY: Very good, that's right, you met her for the first time yesterday. Now, can any of you remember her name?

BILLY: Dolores.

AMY [LAUGHING SLIGHTLY]: No, not Dolores.

MR. BROWNSTEIN: She vas, I caught sight ya know, jussaminute, flahtied or vhat, vhere, midda [HE HUMS A NOTE]—

AMY: Music.

MR. BROWNSTEIN: Yeah right goodgirlie right she vas lissning, I caught slight, saw her vooding bockstond tipping-n-topping de foot vas jussnow like dis. [HE STARTS TO STAMP HIS FOOT]

AMY: Mrs. Stilson, were you inside listening to some music just now?

MRS. STILSON: Well . . .

PAUSE.

[VERY FAST] Well now I was yes in the what in-the-in-the where the—

AMY [CHEERFULLY]: Sssssllllow dowwwwn.

THE OTHER PATIENTS LAUGH; MRS. TIMMINS SOFTLY ECHOES THE PHRASE "SLOW DOWN."

[SPEAKING VERY SLOWLY] Listen to yourself talking.

MRS. STILSON [SPEAKING SLOWLY]: Well yes, I was . . . listening and it was it was going in . . . good I think, I'd say, very good yes I liked it very nice it made it very nice inside.

AMY: Well, good.

MRS. TIMMINS: Applawdgia!

AMY: Ah, Mrs. Timmins! You heard the music, too?

MRS. TIMMINS [WITH A LAUGH]: Ohshorrrrrrn. Yossssso, TV.

AMY: Well, good for you! Anyway, I'd like you all to know that this new person in our group is named Mrs. Stilson.

MR. BROWNSTEIN: Sssssstaa-illlllssssim.

AMY: Right! Well done, Mr. Brownstein!

MR. BROWNSTEIN [LAUGHING PROUDLY]: It's vurktiddiDINGobitch!

AMY: That's right it's working, I told you it would.

BILLY: Hey! Wait, hold on here—jus' remembered!

AMY: What's that, Billy?

BILLY: You've been holdin' out pay up where is it?

AMY: Where . . . is what?

BILLY: Where is for all what I did all that time labor which you—don't kid me, I see you grinning back there ate up [HE MAKES MUNCHING SOUNDS] so where is it, where's the loot?

AMY: For the cheesecake.

BILLY: That's right you know it for the cheesecape, own recipe, extra-special, pay up.

AMY [TO MRS. STILSON]: Billy is a terrific cook.

MRS. STILSON [DELIGHTED]: Oh!

BILLY: Well used t' be, not now much what they say, anyhow, hah-hah! see? look, laughing, giggles, tries t' hide it, she knows she knows, scoundrel, thief, can't sleep nights can you, people give their arms whatnots recipe like that one is. Cheapskate. Come on fork over hand it over, don't be chief.

AMY: . . . What?

BILLY: Don't be chief.

PAUSE.

You know, when someone don' pay, you say he's chief.

AMY [WARMLY, NEARLY LAUGHING]: Billy, you're not listening.

BILLY: Okay not the word not the right word what's the word? I'll take any help you can give me. [HE LAUGHS]

AMY: Cheap.

BILLY: That's it that's the word that's what you are, from now on I'm gonna sell my recipes somewheres else.

AMY: Billy, say cheap.

HE SIGHS MIGHTILY.

BILLY: . . . Chief.

HER EXPRESSION TELLS HIM EVERYTHING.

Not right okay, try again this thing we can, what's its, lessee okay here we go CHARF! Nope. Not right. Ya know really, this could take all day.

AMY: Well then, the sooner you do it, the sooner we can go on to what I've planned.

BILLY: You've got somethin' planned? You've never got somethin' planned.

AMY: I've *always* got something planned.

BILLY: Oh come on don' gimme that, you're jus' tryin' to impress this new lady, really nice new lady, Mrs. . . .

AMY: Stilson.

BILLY: Yeah her, you're jus' tryin'—what's that word again?

AMY: Cheap.

BILLY: Cheap right okay lessee now—

AMY: Billy! You just said it!

BILLY: Did I? Good. Then maybe we can go on to somethin' else, such as when you're gonna fork over for the cheesecake, I could be a rich man now.

AMY: Billy, I never made the cheesecake.

BILLY: I'll bet you've gone sold the recipe to all the stores the whatnot everywhere fancy bigdeal places made a fortune, gonna retire any day t' your farm in New Jersey.

AMY: I don't have a farm in New Jersey, *you* have a farm in New Jersey!

BILLY: Oh? Then what were you doin' on my farm then?

AMY: I wasn't on your farm, Billy, I've been here!
[BILLY STARTS ARGUING ABOUT SOMETHING INCOMPREHENSIBLE AND SEEMINGLY UNRELATED TO FARM LIFE, THE ARGUMENT CONSISTING MOSTLY OF THE RECITATION OF A CONVOLUTED STRING OF NUMBERS; AMY CUTS HIM SHORT BEFORE HE GOES TOO FAR ASTRAY] Billy, cheap, say cheap!

LONG SILENCE.

BILLY [SIMPLY AND WITHOUT EFFORT]: Cheap.

AMY CHEERS.

[OVERJOYED] Cheap!— Cheap-cheap-cheap-cheap-cheap!

MR. BROWNSTEIN: I vas hoping you could polsya and git vid mustard all dis out of dis you gottit right good I say hutchit and congratulupsy!

AMY: Congratu*lations.*

MR. BROWNSTEIN: Yeah right dassit goodgirlie, phhhhew! fin'lly!

LIGHTS FADE TO BLACK ALL AROUND MRS. STILSON. NOTHING SEEN BUT HER.

SILENCE FOR A TIME.

MRS. STILSON: *What it was . . . how I heard it how I said it not the same, you would think so but it's not. Sometimes . . . well it just goes in so fast, in-and-out all the sounds. I know they mean—*

PAUSE.

I mean I know they're . . . well like with me, helping, as their at their in their best way knowing how I guess they practice all the time so I'd say must be good or even better, helps me get the dark out just by going you know sssslowww and thinking smiling . . . it's not easy.

PAUSE.

Sometimes . . . how can . . . well it's just I think these death things, end it, stuff like sort of may be better not to listen anything no more at all or trying even talking cause what good's it, I'm so far away! Well it's crazy I don't mean it I don't think, still it's just like clouds that you can't push through. Still you do it, still you try to. I can't hear things same as others say them.

PAUSE.

So the death thing, it comes in, I don't ask it, it just comes in, plays around in there, I can't get it out till it's ready, goes out on its own. Same I guess for coming. I don't open up the door.

SILENCE.

LIGHTS UP ON A CHAIR, SMALL TABLE.

ON THE TABLE, A CASSETTE RECORDER.

MRS. STILSON GOES TO THE CHAIR. SITS. STARES AT THE RECORDER.

A FEW MOMENTS LATER, BILLY AND A DOCTOR ENTER.

BILLY: Oh, I'm sorry, I didn't know you was in . . . here or . . .

MRS. STILSON: Dr. Freedman said I could . . . use room and his . . . this . . . [SHE GESTURES TOWARD THE RECORDER]

DOCTOR: No problem, we'll use another room.

HE SMILES. EXIT BILLY AND DOCTOR.

MRS. STILSON TURNS BACK TO THE MACHINE. STARES AT IT. THEN SHE REACHES OUT, PRESSES A BUTTON.

DOCTOR'S VOICE [FROM CASSETTE RECORDER]: All right, essentially, a stroke occurs when there's a stoppage . . . When blood flow ceases in one part of the brain . . . And that brain can no longer get oxygen . . . And subsequently dies. Okay? Now, depending upon which part of the brain is affected by the stroke, you'll see differences in symptoms. Now what you've had is a left cerebral infarction. Oh, by the way, you're doing much, much better. We were very worried when you first arrived . . .

SILENCE.

SHE CLICKS OFF THE RECORDING MACHINE. DOES NOTHING, STARES AT NOTHING. THEN SHE REACHES OUT AND PUSHES THE REWIND BUTTON. THE MACHINE REWINDS TO START OF TAPE. STOPS AUTOMATICALLY. SHE STARES AT THE MACHINE. DEEP BREATH. REACHES OUT AGAIN. PRESSES THE PLAYBACK BUTTON.

DOCTOR'S VOICE: All right, essentially, a stroke occurs when there's a stoppage . . . When blood flow ceases in one part of the brain . . . And that brain can no long—

SHE SHUTS IT OFF.

STARES INTO SPACE.

SILENCE.

———————

MRS. STILSON WITH AMY SITTING NEXT TO HER ON ANOTHER CHAIR.

MRS. STILSON [STILL STARING INTO SPACE]: "Memory" . . .

PAUSE.

AMY: Yes, come on, "memory" . . .

NO RESPONSE.

Anything.

STILL NO RESPONSE.

[WARMLY]: Oh, come on, I bet there are lots of things you can talk about . . . You've been going out a lot lately . . . With your son . . . With your niece . . .

PAUSE.

What about Rhinebeck? Tell me about Rhinebeck.

PAUSE.

MRS. STILSON: On . . . Saturday . . . [SHE PONDERS] On . . . Sunday my . . . son . . . [PONDERS AGAIN] On Saturday my son . . . took me to see them out at Rhinebeck.

AMY: See what?

MRS. STILSON: What I used to . . . fly in.

AMY: Can you think of the word?

MRS. STILSON: . . . What word?

AMY: For what you used to fly in.

LONG PAUSE.

MRS. STILSON: Planes!

AMY: Very good!

MRS. STILSON: Old . . . planes.

AMY: That is very good. Really!

MRS. STILSON: I sat . . . inside one of them. He said it was like the kind I used to . . . fly in and walk . . . out on wings in. I couldn't believe I could have ever done this.

PAUSE.

But he said I did, I had. He was very . . . proud.

PAUSE.

Then . . . I saw my hand was pushing on this . . . stick . . . Then my hand was . . . pulling. Well I hadn't you know asked my hand to do this, it just went and did it on its own. So I said okay Emily, if this is how it wants to do it you just sit back here and watch . . . But . . . my head, it was really . . . hurting bad. And I was up here both . . . sides, you know . . .

AMY: Crying.

MRS. STILSON [WITH EFFORT]: Yeah.

LONG PAUSE.

And then all at once—it remembered everything!

LONG PAUSE.

But now it doesn't.

SILENCE.

———————

FAINT SOUND OF WIND. HINT OF BELLS.

THE SCREENS OPEN.

WE ARE OUTSIDE. SENSE OF DISTANCE, OPENNESS.
ALL FEELING OF CONSTRAINT IS GONE. AMY HELPS
MRS. STILSON INTO AN OVERCOAT; AMY IS IN AN
OVERCOAT ALREADY.

AMY: Are you sure you'll be warm enough?

MRS. STILSON: Oh yes . . .

AND THEY START TO WALK—A LEISURELY STROLL
THROUGH A PARK OR MEADOW, SENSE OF WHITENESS
EVERYWHERE. THEY HEAD TOWARD A BENCH WITH
SNOW ON ITS SLATS. THE SOUND OF WIND GROWS
STRONGER.

FAINT SOUND OF AN AIRPLANE OVERHEAD, THE
SOUND QUICKLY DISAPPEARING.

MRS. STILSON: This is winter, isn't it?

AMY: Yes.

MRS. STILSON: That was just a guess, you know.

AMY [WITH A WARM, EASY LAUGH]: Well, it was a good
one, keep it up!

MRS. STILSON LAUGHS.

AMY STOPS BY THE BENCH.

Do you know what this is called?

MRS. STILSON: Bench!

AMY: Very good! No, I mean what's on top of it.

NO RESPONSE.

What I'm brushing off . . .

STILL NO RESPONSE.

What's falling from the sky . . .

LONG SILENCE.

MRS. STILSON: Where do you get names from?

AMY: I? From in here, same as you.

MRS. STILSON: Do you know how you do it?

AMY: No.

MRS. STILSON: Then how am I supposed . . . to learn?

AMY [SOFTLY]: I don't really know.

MRS. STILSON STARES AT AMY. THEN SHE POINTS AT
HER AND LAUGHS.

AT FIRST, AMY DOESN'T UNDERSTAND.

THEN SHE DOES.

AND THEN BOTH OF THEM ARE LAUGHING.

MRS. STILSON: Look. You see? [SHE SCOOPS SOME
SNOW OFF THE BENCH] If I pick this . . . stuff up in my
hand, then . . . I know its name. I didn't have to pick it up to
know . . . what it *was*.

AMY: No . . .

MRS. STILSON: But to find its name . . . [SHE STARES AT
WHAT IS IN HER HAND] I had to pick it up.

AMY: What's its name?

MRS. STILSON: Snow. It's really nuts, isn't it!

AMY: It's peculiar!

THEY LAUGH.

THEN, LAUGHTER GONE, THEY SIT; STARE OUT.

SILENCE FOR A TIME.

MRS. STILSON: A strange thing happened to me . . .

PAUSE.

I think last night.

AMY: Can you remember it?

MRS. STILSON: Perfectly.

AMY: Ah!

MRS. STILSON: I think it may have been . . . you know,
when you sleep . . .

AMY: A dream.

MRS. STILSON: Yes, one of those, but I'm not . . . sure that
it was . . . that.

PAUSE. THEN SHE NOTICES THE SNOW IN HER HAND.

Is it all right if I . . . eat this?

AMY: Yes! We used to make a ball of it, then pour maple
syrup on top. Did you ever do that?

MRS. STILSON: I don't know.

PAUSE.

No, I remember—I did!

SHE TASTES THE SNOW. SMILES.

AFTER A TIME, THE SMILE VANISHES.

SHE TURNS BACK TO AMY.

Who was that man yesterday?

AMY: What man?

MRS. STILSON: In our group. He seemed all right.

AMY: Oh, that was last week.

MRS. STILSON: I thought for sure he was all right! I thought
he was maybe, you know, a doctor.

AMY: Yes, I know.

MRS. STILSON [SEARCHING HER MEMORY]: And you
asked him to show you where his . . . hand was.

AMY: And he knew.

MRS. STILSON: That's right, he raised his hand, he knew.
So I thought, why is Amy joking?

SHE PONDERS.

Then you asked him . . . [SHE TRIES TO REMEMBER] . . .
where . . . [SHE TURNS TO AMY]

AMY: His elbow was.

MRS. STILSON: Yes! And he . . . [SHE STRUGGLES TO
FIND THE WORD]

AMY [HELPING]: Pointed—

MRS. STILSON [AT THE SAME TIME]: Pointed! to . . .[BUT THE STRUGGLE'S GETTING HARDER]

AMY: The corner of the room.

MRS. STILSON: Yes.

PAUSE.

[SOFTLY] That was very . . . scary.

AMY: Yes.

MRS. STILSON STARES INTO SPACE.

SILENCE.

What is it that happened to you last night?

MRS. STILSON: Oh yes! Well, this . . . *person* . . . came into my room. I couldn't tell if it was a man or woman or . . . young or old. I was in my bed and it came. Didn't seem to have to walk just . . . came over to my . . . bed and . . . smiled at where I was.

PAUSE.

And then it said . . . [IN A WHISPER] "Emily . . . we're glad you changed your mind."

PAUSE.

And then . . . it turned and left.

AMY: Was it a doctor? [MRS. STILSON SHAKES HER HEAD] One of the staff? [MRS. STILSON SHAKES HER HEAD] How do you know?

MRS. STILSON: I just know.

PAUSE.

Then . . . I left my body.

AMY: *What?*

MRS. STILSON [WITH GREAT EXCITEMENT]: I was on the
. . . what's the name over me—

AMY: Ceiling?

MRS. STILSON: Yes! I was floating like a . . .

AMY: Cloud?

MRS. STILSON SHAKES HER HEAD.

Bird?

MRS. STILSON: Yes, up there at the—[SHE SEARCHES
FOR THE WORD; FINDS IT]—ceiling, and I looked down and
I was still there in my bed! Wasn't even scared, which you'd
think I would be . . . And I thought, wow! this is the life isn't
it?

SOUND OF WIND.

LIGHTS BEGIN TO CHANGE.

AMY RECEDES INTO THE DARKNESS.

*It comes now without my asking . . . Amy is still beside me
but I am somewhere else. I'm not scared. It has taken me,
and it's clear again. Something is about to happen.*

PAUSE.

AMY NOW COMPLETELY GONE.

MRS. STILSON IN A NARROW SPOT OF LIGHT,
DARKNESS ALL AROUND.

*I am in a plane, a Curtiss Jenny, and it's night. Winter. Snow
is falling. Feel the tremble of the wings! How I used to walk
out on them! Could I have really done— . . . Yes. What I'd
do, I'd strap myself with a tether to the stays, couldn't see
the tether from below, then out I'd climb! Oh my, but it was
wonderful! I could feel the wind! shut my eyes, all alone—
FEEL THE SOARING!*

THE WIND GROWS STRONGER.

THEN THE WIND DIES AWAY.

SILENCE.

SHE NOTICES THE CHANGE.

MRS. STILSON: *But this is in another time. Where I've been
also . . . It is night and no one else is in the plane. Is it . . .
remembering?*

PAUSE.

No . . . No, I'm simply there again!

PAUSE.

*And I'm lost . . . I am lost, completely lost, have to get to . . .
somewhere, Omaha I think. The radio is out, or rather for
some reason picks up only Bucharest. Clouds all around, no
stars only snow, don't possess a clue to where I am, flying
blind, soon be out of gas . . . And then the clouds open up a
bit, just a bit, and lights appear below, faint, a hint, like
torches. Down I drop! heart pounding with relief, with joy,
hoping for a landing place, I'll take anything—a field, a street,
and down I drop! No place to land . . . It's a town but the
smallest—one tiny street is all, three street lamps, no one on
the street, all deserted . . . just a street and some faint light*

in the middle of darkness. Nothing. Still, down I go! Maybe I can find a name on a railroad station, find out where I am! . . . But I see nothing I can read . . . So I begin to circle, though I know I'm wasting fuel and I'll crash if I keep this up! But somehow, I just can't tear myself away! Though I know I should pull back on the stick, get the nose up, head north into darkness—Omaha must be north! But no, I keep circling this one small silly street in this one small town . . . I'm scared to leave it, that's what, as if I guess once away from it I'll be inside something empty, black, and endless . . .

PAUSE.

So I keep circling—madness!—but I love it, what I see below! And I just can't bring myself to give it up, it's that simple— just can't bring myself to give it up!

PAUSE.

Then I know I have to. It's a luxury I can't afford. Fuel is running low, almost gone, may be too late anyway, so—

PAUSE.

I pull the nose up, kick the rudder, bank, and head out into darkness all in terror! GOD, BUT IT TAKES EFFORT! JUST DON'T WANT TO DO IT! . . . But I do.

PAUSE.

[SUDDENLY CALM] *Actually, odd thing, once I did, broke free, got into the dark, found I wasn't even scared . . . Or was I?* [SLIGHT LAUGH] *Can't remember . . . Wonder where that town was . . . ?*

PAUSE.

Got to Omaha all right.

PAUSE.

Was it Omaha . . . ?

PAUSE.

Yes, I think so . . . Yes, Topeka, that was it!

PAUSE.

God, but it was wonderful! [SLIGHT LAUGH] *Awful scary sometimes, though!*

AMY SEEN IN THE DISTANCE.

AMY: Emily! Emily, are you all right!

SUDDEN, SHARP, TERRIFYING FLAPPING SOUND.

MRS. STILSON GASPS.

AMY DISAPPEARS.

MRS. STILSON [RAPIDLY]: *Around! There here spins saw it rumple chumps and jumps outgoes inside up and . . . takes it, gives it, okay . . .*

PAUSE.

[EASIER] *Touch her for me, would you?*

PAUSE.

[EVEN EASIER] *Oh my, yes, and here it goes then out . . . there I think on . . . wings? Yes . . .*

PAUSE.

[SOFTLY, FAINT SMILE] *Thank you.*

NO TRACE OF TERROR.

MUSIC. HINT OF BELLS.

LIGHTS TO BLACK.

SILENCE.